Ballinascreen Gravestone Inscriptions

Straw "old" graveyard

Transcribed and compiled
by
Patrick Kelly and Graham Mawhinney

Foreword
by
Monsignor Joseph Donnelly

Ballinascreen Historical Society, 2008

ISBN 978-0-9544341-5-1

Ballinascreen Historical Society gratefully acknowledges financial
support from Magherafelt Arts Trust and the Community Relations
Department of Magherafelt District Council.

Ballinascreen Historical Society
c/o 7 Tobermore Road,
Draperstown
BT45 7AG

FOREWORD

Once again, the Ballinascreen Historical Society has provided an invaluable service not only to the Parish but to all with an inquiring mind and to anyone interested in tracing their ancestors.

My earliest memory of the old graveyard dates back to my time at Straw School. I can recall pulling myself up to peep over the wall opposite the school to look at the irregular array of headstones. Later, I often stood as an altar server at the graveside during a funeral, always intrigued at the chiselled names and the ancient dates. As the new, more orderly graveyard extended on the other side of the church there was a danger that the old would become a forgotten territory. This publication ensures that this will not happen.

At first glance, the work undertaken may seem a relatively simple task. Anyone who has had to search for a particular grave and has attempted to decipher an inscription, worn away under the erosion of years, will know that the opposite is the case. This is a major achievement. Making 'straight' lines out of a random series of burials, presenting transcriptions with painstaking accuracy and offering intelligent guesses where weathering has erased the original letters, all combine to present us with a publication that will stand the test of time. The beauty of it is that, once it is completed, it is available now for all in the future.

Providing the index to the work was a thoughtful and necessary addition. It will prove an invaluable aid to researchers and to anyone looking for a family name.

As a native of the Parish of Ballinascreen, I welcome this publication. I offer my congratulations to the Society for revealing yet again a little more of the history that rests in our midst.

Joseph Donnelly, P.P.
Omagh.

INTRODUCTION

The Society's 1981 publication – "Ordnance Survey Memoir for the Parish of Ballinascreen 1836-1837" – contained information on the development of the settlement at Draperstown (p.5). *It* [Draperstown] *was founded in 1798 by Laughlin McNamee, a publican, in the following manner. Before 1797 the cattle fair had been always held in the townland of Moneyneany. In that year at one of the fairs, the company in McNamee's tent became quarrelsome over their liquour. Their ideas suddenly received a new turn by one of the drunkards exclaiming that if he had a house at the Crossroads he would "have a comfortable place to take his glass in", upon which after some further altercation another rushed out and leaping on a cart proclaimed to the multitudes that the next fair would be held at the crossroads of Moyheyland. They accordingly resorted thither at the time appointed and immediately Laughlin McNamee removed to it and built the first houses. He also soon established a weekly market by giving free crainage and entertainment and to this day* [1836] *it, as well as the principal part of the fair, is held about his doorway.*

Imagine, then, our excitement and enthusiasm when on a sunny afternoon (and there were a few!) in August 2008, we located the headstone (25) of a Laughlin McNamee in the corner of Straw old graveyard near the main church entrance. With that unusual combination of names, and the dates fitting, we had now, almost certainly found out the dates of death and ages of the founder of Draperstown and his wife Bridget. Such are the joys of "doing" local history and making local connections. It also exemplifies the fact that the recording of gravestone inscriptions is a valuable aid to people with an interest in either local or family history. Gravestone inscriptions can go back long before parish registers commenced and have the extra advantage of often giving other information such as family relationships and ages, which may not occur in the registers.

Moving on 26 years and about 30 publications later, the Society's 2007 publication – "The Schools of Ballinascreen (1823–1990)" – made reference (p.6) to the first Straw school being built in 1834. *The first teacher was Thomas McGowan, who had come from Ballymena to settle down in Straw and who was to teach in Straw for 34 years, to be replaced in 1868 by his son. His wife Ellen was later appointed Work Mistress in the school.* Thomas McGowan's last resting place (51) was discovered a few steps away from Laughlin McNamee's. The intrepid transcribers were, once again, enthused!

Across the graveyard lies Shibbie Kelly (158) after whom Shibby's crossroads, near Straw, gets its name. Also on that side of the graveyard, two out of three moss-covered slabs revealed the names of Rev. Dean Murphy (178) and Rev. Patrick Morgan (179). These, and many others, proved difficult to read and the third (177) of this trio defeated us. We were also pleased to locate the burying place of Rev. Patrick M'Glade (189) who died in 1843, but apparently little else is known about him.

It was also interesting to note that local stone masons were evident, with the name H. Mallaghan on one headstone (32) and F. Quigley, Ballynure on two others (29, 39). It was surprising to note that few inscriptions included a townland and only one made a, even oblique, reference to a nickname (19). The quality of the lettering varied a great deal and the workmanship on some of the earlier ones was primitive. In many cases the sculptor would run out of space in the middle of a name, word or date and the remaining letters or figures were just carried over to the next line. To complicate matters further there were many variations of spellings of surnames and common words and occasionally there were just obvious spelling blunders (see, for example, 108).

All spellings are given as they are on the stone. However, the peculiarities of the styles of "Mac" surnames – for example M'Kenna, M,Kenna, McKenna, McKenna or McKenna – have been standardised to the latter. Where surnames begin with a lower case letter, this is preserved. So, for example, we have names like mcEldowney, or mcGugin. Some modern punctuation has been added or attempted, to add clarity. Headstones are indicated by H and horizontal slabs by S. The gravestones are not, of course, arranged in neat lines but for our purposes we tried to subdivide them into rough rows. The first and last number of each row is indicated on the accompanying sketch plan. We have used the following notation in our transcriptions:-

(   ) uncertain words or figures
[   ] inscription missing or not visible, but inserted missing words or figures
..... illegible words or figures.

Even though the "summer" of 2008 will long be remembered as one of the wettest on record, we did take every opportunity to check and re-check our efforts. However, with old stones such as many of these, there will often be doubts and differences of opinion. We anticipate that errors may have slipped through and we sincerely apologise for them.

We would wish to thank Joe Conville for practical assistance. His help in lifting and cleaning damaged headstones was much appreciated. We also offer thanks to Monsignor Joseph Donnelly, a native of Labby, for contributing the foreword and to Susan Potter, our talented and patient typesetter.

Transcribing headstones in a graveyard may not be everyone's favourite pastime, but we thoroughly enjoyed the project and maybe, God willing, we will proceed to transcribe others. On most of the headstones the wording follows a fairly standard pattern, but occasionally there is a surprise. Headstone 128 displays this sombre, but clever, little verse –

Absent or dead, still let a friend be dear
A sigh the absent claim, the dead a tear.

Patrick Kelly
Graham Mawhinney

ROW 1

1. Dennis McCartney, died August 9th 1835, aged 36 years. Requiescat in Pace.   H

2. Headstone – no visible inscription.

3. IHS. Erected in memory of Edward Kelly who departed this life 14 April 1817 aged (70) years.   S

4. IHS. Erected by John Bradley in memory of his wife Ann Bradley who departed this life 23rd Feb 1850 aged 31 years.   Also his son Michael who departed this life 6th Nov 1862 aged 26 years.   Pray for the soul of above John Bradley who died 3rd August 1881 aged 95 years.   S

5. IHS. Erected in memory of Cormick O'Neill who died … June 1863 aged 82 years. His wife Ann O'Neill died 20 April 1840 aged 70. His son Michael died 18 April 1819 aged (30) years. His daughter Mary died 1 March 1839 aged 50 years.   S

6. IHS. In memory of Alice Devlin died 10th April 1932, her husband James died 9th March 1934 and their daughter Alice died 4th August 1947. RIP. Erected by their daughter Mary and son-in-law George Hopper(Canada) H

7. IHS. In memory of Michael Duffy who died 12th July 1854 aged 66 years. Also his wife Alice who died 12 July 1844 aged 34 years.   H(against wall)

8. IHS. In loving memory of Michael Duffy died 12th July 1854, Alice (Kelly) Duffy died 12th July 1844, Patrick Duffy died Easter Sunday 1881, Ann (Kelly) Duffy died 3rd May 1906, Thomas Hegarty died 25th January 1897, Catherine (Duffy) Hegarty died 14th June 1930, Patrick Hegarty died 10th April 1997. RIP   H

9. Of your charity pray for the souls of John McKeown who died 20 Oct 1891, James McKeown died 28 July 1910, his wife Mary died 22 Dec 1907 and their children Joseph died 21 Dec 1898, Mary died 26 Nov 1909, Anthony died 21 March 1921, Daniel died 26 Apr 1942, Peter died 8 Dec 1961.   H

10. IHS. Erected in memory of Michael McKeown [who] departed this life 10th October 1867 aged 26 years.
         H(against wall)

11. IHS. McKeown. In loving memory of Hugh McKeown died 24th Nov 1979. RIP.   H

12. IHS. Erected by his loving wife and family in memory of James O'Connor who died 3 Oct 1922. Also his daughters Anne and Jeannie. Also his father and mother Henry O'Connor who died June 14 1878 aged 65 years. Also Bridget O'Connor who died in 1900 aged 84 years. And also his sister Annie.   H(against wall, broken)

13. IHS. Sacred to the memory of John Henery who departed this life January the 21st 1818 aged 69 years. Also Alice Henery wife of the above who departed this life August the 7th 1817 aged 59 years.   H

14. Stone surround – no inscription.

15. IHS. Mary Henery died April 3rd 1828 aged (58) years, Edward Henry died June 28th 1845 aged 68 years, Daniel Henry died 15th April 1849 aged 77 years   S

ROW 2

16. IHS. Rev. Daniel Magee. ADMINISTRATOR HACEE DE CURA. NATUS 1821. OBIIT 1881. HOMINI BONO IN CONSPECTU SUO DEUS DEDIT SAPIENTIAM ET SCIENTIAM ET LAETITIAM. Eccl. c.2 "Requiescat in Pace"   H

17. IHS. Erected by Hugh McConnel in memory of his mother Rose Kelly who dept this life Dec 8th 1839 aged 63 years.   H

18. IHS. This stone was erected by his son Edward Kelly in memory of his father James Kelly who dept this life March 4th 1823 aged 77 years, also his wife Hannah Kelly otherwise Murry who died June 8th 1823 aged 65 years.   H

19. Kelly(N) Labby. Erected in memory of Neil Kelly died 20th Jan 1902, his wife Brigid died 15th March 1904, their son Michael died 14th August 1908 and his wife Mary died 23rd March 1956, their grand daughters Kathleen died 1st Feb 1982, Brigid died 28th Aug 1987, their great grandchildren John, Thomas and Magdeline who died in infancy. RIP   H

20. IHS. no inscription – iron rail surround only

21. IHS. Here lieth the body of ....McGillian who dep. this life August the 20th 1817 aged ...... years. Also his wife Bridget.   H

22. IHS. Erected in memory of Charles O'Hagan who departed this life 22nd Nov 1864 aged 55 years. Also his wife Bridget who died 3rd March 1888 aged 80 years.   H

23. IHS. Connor. Sacred heart of Jesus have mercy on the souls of James Connor died 3rd Oct 1922, his wife Mary died 24th Oct 1923, his parents Henry died 14th June 1879, Bridget died 6th June 1900, his sons Harry died 20th April 1975, Peter died 30th Jan 1976, Jennie died 10th Dec 1985, Nellie died 19th April 1986.   H

24. Concrete base – no inscription.

25. Here lieth the body of Bridget McNamee who departed this life Jan 19th 1825 aged 65 years. Also her husband Laughlin McNamee who died 12th June 1813 aged 83 years.   H

ROW 3

26. IHS. Here lieth the body of Mary O'Kelly who depd. this
    life Sept 15 1818 aged 36 years.   H

27. IHS. Here lieth the body of Bryan Kelly who depd. this
    life 16th Nov.br. 1833 aged 72 years. Also his wife[ ] H

28. In memory of Michael O'Neill who died Novr. 25th 1870
    aged 61 years. Also his son John who died 6th April 1895
    aged 50 years. Jane O'Neill died 27th Sep. 1909 aged 87
    years. Also his daughter Bridget McAllister died 9th
    November 1926 aged 78 years. Her grandson Sean
    McAllister died 27th Dec 2005 aged 73 years.
    Requiescent in Pace   Amen.   H

29. Erected by Bernard Rogers in memory of his son James
    who died 6th May 1882 aged 22 years. For whose soul of
    your charity pray. And that of the above Bernard Rogers
    who died 17th May 1895 aged 81 years. Also Bridget the
    wife of Bernard who died 25th Decr. 1899 aged 72 yrs.
    F. Quigley, Ballynure.   H

30. Pray for the soul of James Bradley who died 17th March
    1863 aged 76 years. Also of Mary Bradley alias Clarke
    his daughter who died 23rd January 1865 aged 38 years.
    Also Ann Bradley his daughter who died 26th June 1877
    aged 35 years.   H

31. Erected in memory of Michael Bradley who departed this
    life May the 15th 1858 aged 36 years.   H

32. IHS. Erected in memory of Francis Bradley who died June 6th 1853 aged 26 years and his mother Rose Moran who died March 2nd 1876 aged 80 years.
H. Mallaghan   H

33. IHS. In loving memory of Bridget wife of Joseph McNamee of Glengamna who died 20th August 1881 aged 70 years and of his children Peter who died 12th Nov 1837 aged 1 year, Anthony who died 20th Nov 1846 aged 3 years, Susan who died 25th Dec. 1846 aged 16 years and Anthony who died 29th April 1880 aged 31 years.
Requiescent in Pace. Amen.   H

34. IHS. Erected by Daniel Reed to the memory of his father Paul who depd. this life 30th May 1830 in the 75th year of his life.   S(leaning against wall)

ROW 4

35. IHS. Erected by Peter McKenna in memory of his father Daniel who died on the 26th February 1871 aged 86 years. Also the above named Peter died 17th Novr. 1891 aged 74 years. Also Rose Doogan wife of his nephew Daniel died 19th March 1891 aged 45 yrs.
Annie McKenna died 7th July 1929
Margt. McKenna died 29th March 1933
Daniel McKenna died 29th Oct 1935
Grace McKenna died 8th Oct 1985   H

36. IHS. Moyheeland. Erected by Daniel McKenna in memory of his daughter Alice who died 11th Septr. 1887 aged 21 years. Also his son Francis who died 23rd July 1895 aged 35 years. The above mentioned Daniel McKenna died 23 Oct 1905 aged 96 yrs. His daughter Mary McKenna died 15 March 1908 aged 43 yrs. James McKenna died 29th Jan 1934 aged 84 yrs. His wife Alice Anne died 30th Nov 1956 aged 83 yrs. Also Jim McKenna died 28th Nov 1942 aged 11 yrs. H

37. IHS. Kelly. In loving memory of Daniel Kelly and his wife Rose. Also their daughter Susan and their sons James, John and Michael. RIP H

38. IHS. Erected by John Bradley in memory of his mother Catherine Bradley who died 24th March 1888 aged 55 years. Also her son Patrick Bradley who died 12th Septem. 1883 aged 27 years. H

39. IHS. Erected by James McBride, St Louis, Mo., USA in memory of his mother Margaret McBride (alies) Lynch who died Jany. 8th 1889 aged 70 yrs. Also his father Daniel McBride who died 11th October 1894 aged 83 years. RIP
F. Quigley, Ballynure H

40. [   ] BROKEN HEADSTONE   wife Brigid Bradley died 29 April 1946.   RIP

ROW 5

41. IHS. Of your charity pray for the souls of Elizabeth Harbison McKenna who died 6th October 1882 and of James Timony McKenna who died 14th February 1884. RIP. James J. Alphonsus McKenna who died 15th April 1908. Erected in loving remembrance of his father and mother by his son James Joseph Alphonsus McKenna.   S

42. Kelly. In memory of James died 1st Dec 1909 aged 68 years. His wife Anne died 12th April 1925 aged 97 years. Their son Patrick died 15th Aug 1883 aged 7 years. Their grandson John died 20th Jan 1919 aged 11 months. RIP Straw.   H

43. IHS. McAllister. In loving memory of John McAllister (David) Cahore died 9th July 1938 aged 43 years.   H

44. IHS. Erected by John Lagan, Moneymore in memory of his aunts Sally and Mary Kelly of Bancran. On their souls Sweet Jesus have mercy. RIP.   H

45. IHS. In loving memory of Francis Mallon died 12th March 1888 and his wife Catherine died 1st Novr. 1868. His son John died 5 Octr. 1922 and his daughter Margaret died 22 March 1889. RIP.
Erected by Charles Campbell 6th Aug 1927.   H

46. IHS. To the memory of Bridget wife of James Heron who departed this life 8th Feb 1863 aged 70 years.   H

47. IHS. Erected in memory of Patrick Bradley who departed this life November the 3rd 1857 aged 55 years. Also his daughter Rose who died March 16th 1862 aged 21 years. Peter Bradley who died 20th January 1920 aged 76 years. His wife Matilda who died 4th September 1923 aged 60 years. Also their son Joseph who died 11th September 1964 aged 72 years.   H

48. In memory of Patrick Bradley, Bracka. who died 3rd Nov 1857 aged 55 years. His wife Ann who died 18th Oct 1901 aged 87 years and their son John who died 6th Jan 1897 aged 53 years. Rose Rogers died 3rd June 1921 aged 31 years. Ann Bradley died 24th April 1953 aged 90 years. Her great grandson Owen Kelly who died 10th July 1955 aged 4 months.   RIP
O'Neill & Co., Belfast   H

49. IHS. In loving memory of Jane Kelly who died 10th April 1892. Also her husband John Kelly who died 18th August 1902 and their sons Matthew who died 24th October 1903, Bernard who died 4th January 1900. Also their son-in-law John Cauley who died 13th September 1907. RIP.   H

50. IHS. (Erected) in memory of Peter Kelly who departed this life 14th November 1878 aged (8)6. Also his wife Ellenor Kelly who died 30th April 1882 aged 77 years. Requiescent in Pace.   S

51. IHS. Sacred to the memory of Thomas McGowan, Straw who departed this life 28th May 1880 aged 72 years. Also his wife Ellen died 1st Nov 1890 aged 84 years. Also his sons Edward, Deniss and John and his grandson Eddie who died respectively June 1839, June 1851, December 1852, September 1879.   H

52. IHS. Erected by Daniel Kelly in memory of his mother Susan Kelly who departed this life 19th May 1863 aged 92 years.   H(leaning against wall)

53. .... ILLEGIBLE   H(leaning against wall)

54. IHS. Erected by Pat Crilly in memory of Daniel Hennry who died 11th Jany. 1891 aged 81 yrs. Also Pat Hennry who died in July 187(1) aged 66 yrs.   H(leaning against wall)

ROW 6(Short row)

55. IHS. To the memory of Henry Morren who died 28 June 1838 aged 70 yrs. Also his wife Marthew Hagan who died 26 Feby 1831 aged 60 yrs.   H

56. IHS. Here lieth the body of James Kerr who depd. this life Novr 12th 1831 aged 77 yrs. Also Elizabeth Kerr who depd this life April 15th 1839 aged 46 yrs. Also his son Richard who died April 25 1876 aged 77 years. Requiescant in Pace.   H

57. Erected by James Timony in affectionate remembrance of his daughter Susan McKenna (alias Timony) who departed this life 15th November 1842 aged 26 years. Also his son James Timony who died 29 June 1891 aged 78 yrs. Also his son James' wife Rose Timony died 25th Sepd. 1891 aged 61 yrs. Margaret Timony died 2nd March 1902, Matthew Timony died 13th April 1902, James Timony died 30th Aug 1965, Frank Timony died 16th June 2003.   H

57A IHS. Here lies the body of Hana Timony who depd. this life June the 1 1881 aged 75 yrs. Erected by Francis and James Timony in memory of their father and mother. Matthew Timony who depd. this life 1st March 1837 aged 89 years.   H(lying on grave 57)

58. IHS. Erected by Dominick Crilly in memory of his sons Patrick, died 3rd Sep 1916 interred in USA and Joseph died 27th Feb 1930. Also his wife Mary Crilly died 11th Oct 1933 aged 72 years. The above named Dominick Crilly died 17th April 1935 aged 81 years.   H

59. IHS. Erected by Patrick McKenna in memory of his wife Alice McKenna who departed this life 19th July 1870 aged 76 years. The above named Patrick McKenna who departed this life 21st January 1891 aged 92 years.   H

60. IHS. Peter Duffy died 28th March 1855 aged 36 years. Mary his wife died 13th March 1854 aged 35 years.   S

61. Erected in memory of Dr Francis Carleton JP who died 31st March 1895 aged 80 years. Also his wife Matilda who died 12th Feb 1890 aged 75 years. Also of his son James who died at Arcachon 5th April 1882 aged 30 years and of his son Peter who died 6th December 1923 aged 70 years. Also his son Major Patrick Carleton who died 9th June 1943. RIP.
Also his daughter Teresa Carleton who died 3rd July 1946.
Robinson Belfast   H

62. IHS. Erected by Peter Duffy to the memory of his son Pat^{k} who depd. this life 3rd Nov 1829 aged 19 years. Also his son Bernard who depd. this life 26th June 1853 aged 25 years. Also his son James who depd. this life 1st Sept 1824 aged 1 year.   S

63. IHS. Erected to the memory of Miles Kelly who depd. this life on the 12th March 1845 aged 80 years. Also his daughter Ann who died on the 10 May 1844 aged 24 yrs.
                                                     S

ROW 7

64. IHS. Here lieth the body of Mary McDavit other ways Haron who dpd. this life August the 6th 1822 aged 42 yrs. Also her two sons.   H

65. Gloria in Excelsus Deo (crucifixion scene)
Here lieth the body of James Murray who depd this life May 6 1816 aged 77 yrs. Also Mary Murray who depd. this life March 17 1822 aged 23 yrs.   H

66. IHS. Erected in memory of Michael Murray who depd. this life 2nd June 1853 aged 32 years. Also his four sisters.

                                                   H

67. IHS. Erected by Michael Doyle in memory of his wife Unity Doyle died 13th May 1880 aged 67 years. John Doyle died 4th Jan 1984 aged 95 years. His wife Elizabeth died 11th Oct 1990 aged 95 years.   H
In loving memory of John Doyle died 4th Jan 1984 and his wife Elizabeth died 11th Oct 1990.
Rest in Peace.   PLAQUE ON GRAVE

68. IHS. This stone was erected by Richard Doyle in memory of his two sons Francis who depd. this [life] Febry. 20th 1823 aged 19 ye[a]r[s]. Richard Doyle who died March 10th 1823 ag[e]d 22 yrs.   H

69. IHS. In loving memory of Patrick O'Kane died 27th Feb. 1919 and his wife Annie died 29th May 1929. Also their family:-Ellen, Mary, Catherine, Margaret, Joseph, Patrick and Elizabeth. Also Mary died 23rd Jan 1979. RIP
Watterson.   H

70. IHS. Erected in memory of John McNally who departed this life 1st August 1867 aged 83 years.   S

71. IHS. Erected in memory of James McNally who departed this life 20th June 1860 aged 62 years.   S

72. IHS. Here lieth the body of Eleanor Loughran wife of Michael Loughran who dep. this life April the (11th) 1821 aged 61 years.
Here lieth the body of Michael Loughran who depd. this life January the 7th 1822 aged 25 yrs.   S

73. Here lieth the body of Michael Loughran who departed this life June 30 1823 aged ....   S

74. IHS. In memory of Peter O'Hagan who died on the 6th May 1822 aged 58 years and his wife Susan Convery who died on the 16th October 1857 aged 76 years.   S

75. IHS. Here lieth the body of Hugh O'Kane who depd. this life 28th Oct. 1841 aged 81 years. Also his wife Bridget O'Kane (alias) Convery who depd. this life 1st March 1837 aged 70 yrs. Also their son Hugh who died 2nd Decr. 1879 aged 68 yrs.   H

ROW 8

76. In memory of Daniel Trainor who died July 11th 1883 aged 13 years.   H

77. Erected by Patrick McNicholl New York in remembrance of his parents Patrick McNicholl who died 7th August 1888, Mary McNicholl who died 27th July 1889. Also their children Michael, John & Ellen.   H

78. Here lieth the body of Charles Bradley who depd. this life the 15th of May 1812 aged 21 years. Also Margeret Bradley who dpd. this life the 10th March 1826 aged 80 yrs.   H

79. IHS. Here lieth the body of Catherine Lenon otherwise Cambel who dep. this life April the 20th 1812 aged 50 yrs.
                                                                          H

80. SMALL STONE PILLAR – NO INSCRIPTION

81. IHS. Erected in memory of Sarah Donnelly who died May 29th 1880 aged 24 years. Also her father James Donnelly who died 4th Octr. 1885 aged 75 years. Also his wife Ellen who died 18th Octr. 1890 aged 76 years.   H

82. IHS. Edward Convery who died 20th June 1860 aged 90 years. Also his wife Hanna Convery who died 10th June 1854 aged 85 years. Erected by their son Edward Convery.   H

83. IHS. Erected by Neal Devlin in memory of his wife Rose Devlin who died 14th December 1883 aged 75 years. Also his mother Ann Devlin who died 8th August 1860 aged 80 years.   H

84. CELTIC CROSS TOP IS BROKEN OFF.
Erected by John Boyle in memory of his wife Susan Boyle
who died 17th Dec. 1890 aged 54 yrs. Also his daughters
Mary died 6th July 1887 aged 19 yrs.
Alice died 1st Feb 1889 aged 19 yrs.
Patrick died 1st June 1901 aged 36 yrs.
James died 10th July 1900 aged 29 yrs.   H

85. Here lieth the body of Isabella Kelly who depd. this life
15th July 1897 aged 33 yrs. Also Mary Kelly who depd.
this life 30 April 1893 aged 19 yrs.   S

ROW 9
86. Thy will be done.
Erected by their children Elizabeth & Agnes Devlin,
Philadelphia U.S.A. in memory of their sister Mary Ann
Devlin died 4th Sept. 1884, their sister Sarah died 9th May
1893. Also their father Patrick Devlin died 21st June 1907
and their mother Sarah Devlin died 6th June 1913.
O! Sacred Heart of Jesus have mercy on them. Also their
brother Patrick Devlin died at New York 1903.   H

87. IHS. In memory of Laurence Bradley who departed this
life 6th Dec. 1868 aged 68 years.   H

88. In loving memory of Charles Trolan died 10th Feb. 1919.
His wife Ann died 28th April 1957. Also his parents
Patrick and Bridget. His brothers Michael, Francis and
James and his cousin Minnie Crilly died 30th Dec. 1897.
FLOWER HOLDER – Trolan, Cahore.   H

89. IHS. Erected in memory of James Trolan who died 17th Feb. 1860 aged 36 years. Also his son Michael Trolan who died April 3rd 1892 aged 36 years. His wife Brigid who died 1898, his daughter Mary who died 9th July 1931. RIP.   H

90. IHS. Here lieth the body of Catharine Mccloskey who depd. this life. Also her daughter Eliz^h Mccloskey who depd. this life April 27 1823 aged 18 years.   H

91. Erected by John Clerkin in memory of his daughter Catherine Clerkin who depd. this life 28th August 1870 aged 20 yrs. Also Eliza Clerkin who depd. this life 20 August 1860 aged 22 yrs.   S

92. IHS. Erected by Joseph and Susan Leadon in memory of his wife Rose Leadon who died March 4th 1867 aged 42 years. Also John Leadon who died Sept. 2nd 1875 aged 56 years. Also Mary Leadon who died March 9th 1878 aged 61 years. Also Joseph Leadon who died May 6th 1882 aged 63 years.   H
METAL PLAQUE – Erected in memory of John Leyden died 4th Sept. 1906 and his wife Ellen died 18th Nov. 1927. RIP.

93. Erected by Charles Mury in memory of Petre Mury who died 5 February 1845 aged 73 years. Also his wife Mary Mury who died 12 December 1849 aged 72 years.

94. Erected in memory of John Murry who died August 24 1859 aged 42 years. Also his mother Margret Murry who died August 25 1837 aged 58 years.   H

ROW 10

95. Thy will be done.
    Erected by Martin Gormley in memory of his father Bernard Gormley who died 28th Feb. 1895. Also his mother Catherine Gormley who died 9th June 1919. His sister Rose Gormley who died 17th July 1914. Also James, Catherine and Margaret. RIP.   H

96. Erected by Susan Convery in memory of her father and mother John and Jane Convery and her brother Bernard. RIP.   H

97. In memory of McEldowney family, Derrynoid. RIP   H

98. Erected by the Revd. John O'Doherty at the request of John Bradley in memory of his affectionate father Patrick Bradley who departed this life May 12th 1812 aged 56 years. Also his mother Martha Bradley who departed this life July 8th 1832 aged 75 years and his brother Andrew Bradley who departed this life May 10th 1824 aged 32 years.   H

99. IHS. Here lieth the body of Rose mcEldowney otherways Gallagher who departed this life 1st of Febry. 1812 aged 56 yrs.   H

100. Erected by John McNamee, Glengamna in memory of his beloved son Rev. James McNamee C.C. Ballascullion, Bellaghy who died 14th April 1878 aged 41 years. Requescant in Pace. H

101. IHS. Erected in memory of John McNamee who died 10th January 1880 aged 81 years. Also his wife Anne McNamee who died 25th July 1865 aged 56 years. Requiescant in Pace. H

102. IHS. Erected in memory of Denis Brown who departed this life Feby. 20th 1862 aged 85 yrs. Also his wife Bridget Brown who departed this life 26th August 1858 aged 77 yrs. H

103. IHS. Erected in memory of Edward McAnally who died 15th August 1840 aged 77 yrs. Also his wife Martha McAnally (alias) Conlin who died 22nd March 1841 aged 76 yrs. H

104. SMALL STONE – NO INSCRIPTION

ROW 11

105. Erected by Henry McCullough to the memory of his dearly beloved wife Mary McCullough who departed this life 30th day of October 1886 aged 26 years. Requiesant in Pace. H

106. Thy will be done. Jesus Mercy Mary Help.
Erected in memory of Patrick Moran who died 30th April
1885. Also his wife Mary Moran who died 30th May 1898,
Michael Moran died 7th January 1931, Patrick Moran died
21st March 1932, James Moran died 10th December 1934.
May they rest in peace.   H (broken)

107. IHS. Erected in memory of Bridget Haughey who died 21st
Feby. 1874 aged 44 years and Patrick Haughey died 7th
Feby. 1893 aged 21 years. RIP.   H

108. IHS. Erected by Frank Mcledowney of Derrynoid to the
memory of his sons. Here lieth the body of Francis who
depd. this life March 3rd 1842 aged 21 years. Also Bernard
who depd. this life Feby. the 9th 1844 aged 25 years.   H

109. IHS. Here lieth the body of Elizabeth Donnolly alias Kelly
who depd. this life July the 6th in the year of our lord 1812
aged 50 yrs. Also Andrew Donnelly who died 23rd Janu.
1913 aged 97 years.   H

110. IHS.   Erected by Daniel Henry in memory of his father
Charles Henry who died 22nd August 1861 aged 77 years.
Also his mother Bridget Henry who died 25th of May 1879
aged 81 years. Also his daughter Bridget Henry who died
7th June 1890 aged 20 years.   H

111. IHS. In memory of John Kerr who died 19th July 1872 aged 76 years. Also of Nancy his wife who died 19th Decr. 1860 aged 85 years. Also of Izabella their daughter who died 1st June 1865 aged 28 years. Also Richard Kerr who died 18th Janu. 1912 aged 85 years.   H

112. IHS. Toner. Pray for the Soul of John Toner died 17th Oct. 1932 and his wife Bridget died 6th July 1960. Their daughters Mary Bradley died 17th April 1974, Agnes Dunbar died 3rd March 1981. RIP.   H

113. IHS. Brown. In loving memory of Peter Brown died 3rd Dec. 1903. His wife Catherine died 25th Jan. 1947, their daughter Catherine died 16th Oct. 1966, also their son John died 27th July 1968. RIP.   H

ROW 12

114. IHS. In memory of Matilda Browne who departed this life the 20th of December 1848 aged 28 years.   H

115. IHS. The burying place of the Lennon family of Ballynure.   H

PLAQUE – Pray for the Soul of Annie Bradley, Cloughfin died 13th March 1975.

116. IHS. Erected in memory of Brian Duffy of Goles who died 1st of February 1872 aged 77 years. Also his daughter Sarah who died 3rd May 1851 aged 21 years.   S

117. IHS. Erected by John McCloskey in memory of his wife
Bridget McCloskey who depd. this life 21st Aug. 1841 aged
44 years. John McCloskey died 4th Sept. 1844 aged 86 yrs.
Also Catherin McEldowne[y] who died 17th Dec. 1916
aged 35 yrs. Also her husband Michael McEldowney who
died 4th Jan. 1926.

H

118. IHS. Pray for the soul of Edward McCloskey of
Moneyneena who departed this life May 29th 1881 aged 51
years. RIP.
Erected by his daughter Mary, Philadelphia. H

119. McCormick. RIP. H

120. IHS. Erected by Maria Clarkin of London in memory of
her beloved husband Charles Clarkin who departed this life
September the 7th 1866 aged 51 years. May he rest in
peace. S

121. Erected by Joseph McNamee in loving memory of his
mother Susan McNamee who died 7th Dec. 1930 aged 91
yrs. Also his father Patrick McNamee who died 7th Nov.
1882, aged 40 yrs and their children Michael died 29th Feb.
1952 aged 81 yrs, Patrick died 27th Dec. 1952 aged 77 yrs,
Joseph died 4th June 1954 aged 81 yrs, Catherine died 13th
March 1973 aged 91 yrs. Mary Anne and John interred in
USA. Glengamna. RIP. McNamee
Kennedy, Belfast H

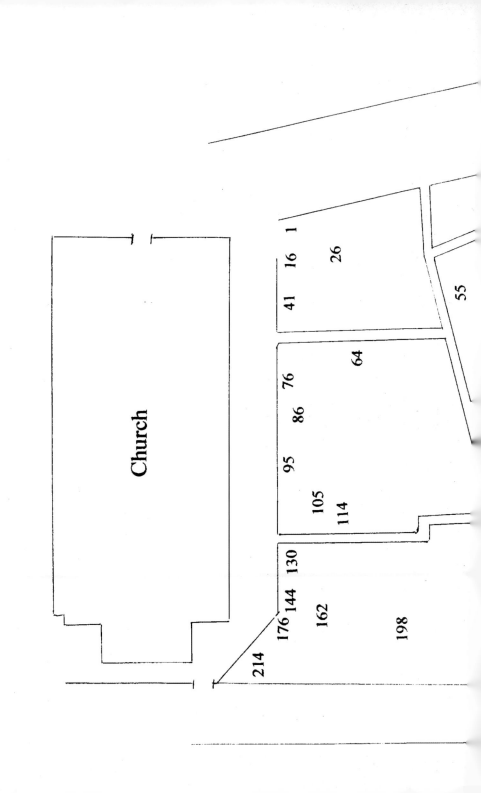

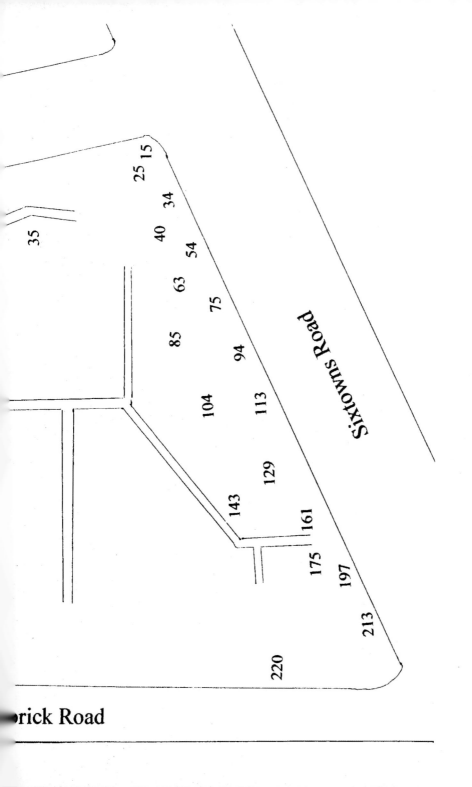

Sixtowns Road

Brick Road

15
25
34
40
54
63
75
85
94
104
113
129
143
161
175
197
213
220
35

122. IHS. This tomb was erected in memory of Charles Conway who depd. this life November the 4th 1822 aged 64 yrs. Also his wife Ann Conway alias Kelly who depd. this life February the 7th 1834 aged 76 yrs.   S

123. IHS. Erected by James Quigley in memory of his father James Quigley who died on the 4th May 1834 . . . . . . Requiescat in Pace.   S

124. JHS. Underneath rest the remains of Mary, daughter of Patrick Henery of Maghera who depd. this life 7th Sept. 1831 aged 11 years.   S(broken)

125. Henry, Pray for the souls of Charles Henry died April 30 1901, his wife Alice died Aug. 13 1927, their daughter-in-law Catherine d. Dec. 13 1975 and her husband Arthur died Oct. 29 1978. RIP.   H

126. IHS. Erected in memory of Nancy Moore. Also her daughter Martha Moore who died 19th July 1898 aged 62 years.   H

127. IHS. Erected in memory of Edward O'Hagan who departed this life 16th March 1856 aged 76 years. Also Mary Ann O'Hagan wife of his son Francis who died 10th March 1892 aged 69 years. Also his wife Susan O'Hagan who died on the 9th May 1864 aged 73 years.   H

128. Erected by John Heron in memory of his wife Mary Heron alias Laughlin who died May 24 1832 aged 40 years. Also his son Henry John who died in 1830 aged 1 year.
REVERSE SIDE – IHS. John Heron's burying place
Absent or dead, still let a friend be dear
A sigh the absent claim, the dead a tear.   H

129. IHS. Erected by John McGlynn in memory of his wife Ann who died 23rd January 1831 aged 75 years.   S

ROW 13

130. In memory of Michael Kelly who died 4th Nov. 1884 aged 86 years. Also his wife Isabella who died 21st Feb. 1857 aged 48 years. Also their son James Kelly who died 3rd Dec. 1919 aged 72 years and his wife Margaret Kelly who died 26th Dec. 1926 aged 81 years.   RIP.
Also Michael Kelly son of James Kelly who died 31st July 1928 aged 52 years. His wife Mary who died 22nd Aug. 1968 aged 79 years. Also two grandchildren Michael Francis and Thomas who died at Belfast. Michael J. Cleary who died in infancy 15th June 1948.
Kelly.   H

131. IHS. Here lieth the body of Hugh O'Neill who depd. this life January the 28 1817 aged 46 yrs.   H

132. IHS. Erected by Bernard Gillespie in memory of his mother Ellen Gillespie. Also his daughter Catherine McGurk who died 27th Septr. 1872 aged 32 years.   H

133. IHS. Erected by James O'Neill in memory of his daughter Catherine who died 17th March 1862 aged 16 years and his son John O'Neill who died 11th April 1932.   H

134. IHS. Here lie the remains of Phelix O'Neill who died 28th Aug. 1825 aged 92. Also Elizabeth his wife died 30th Jany. 1827 aged 86. Also their son Owen who died 11th March 1825 aged 43 years.   S

135. IHS. Erected in memory of Paul O'Neill who died 2nd March 1863 aged 67 years.   H

136. IHS. Here lieth the body of William O'Kane who depd. this life Nov. the 9th 1812 agd. 79 yrs. Also his wife Eleanor O'Kane who depd. Feby. the 13th 1818 agd. 77 yrs.   H

137. In memory of Michael Toner who died 2nd April 1871 aged 77 years.   S

138. IHS. Here lieth the body of Bryan Toner who depd. this life 13th Jan. 1829 aged 65 yrs.   H

139. Here lieth the body of John Toner who dpd. this life July the 1th 1818 aged 62 yrs.   H

140. METAL PLAQUE ON METAL RAIL – Burial place of John Toner and family.

141. IHS. Thy will be done. Erected by the late Revd. James McGuigan PP. Kilrea to the memory of his father, mother, brothers & sisters.   H

142. Erected by Francis Clerkin in memory of his wife Mary Clerkin who depd. this life the 23rd April 1855 aged 50 years. Also his son Michael who departed this life the 15th June 1855 aged 12 years.   H

143. IHS. Erected in memory of James Crawley who died 16th Septr. 1851 aged 69 years.   H

ROW 14

144. IHS. Erected by Henry McCullough in memory of his brother Patrick McCullough died 20th June 1881 aged 22 years. Isabella McCullough died Oct. 1904. Charles died April 1927. Their son Henry died Oct. 1957. His father John McCullough died 26th Nov. 1898 aged 92 years. Also his mother Susan McCullough died 15th Feb. 1899 aged 84 years.   H

145. In memory of Bridget O'Neill who departed this life November the 4th 1860 aged 36 years. Also John O'Neill who died July 10th 1868 aged 63 years.   H

146. IHS. Erected by John Kelly in memory of his mother Catharine who departed this life 29th May 1864 aged 78 years. Also his wife Mary who died 2nd Decr. 1891 aged 68 years.   H

147. In loving memory of Agnes Kelly (nee Cullinan) Doon died 11th November 1915. Her husband James died 23rd December 1918. Their son John died March 1934. Their son Patrick Oliver died 26th September 1984. Rest in Peace. Kelly.   H

148. IHS. Francis O'Neill died 24th March 1834 aged 54. Bridget his wife 1st November 1860 aged 74. Their son Bernard 9th April 1860 aged 34 years. Their son Gordon John 10th July 1877 aged 44.   H

149. IHS. Thy will be done.
In memory of Patrick O'Neill Dysart who died 16th April 1870. Also his wife Mary O'Neill who died 23rd Sep. 1899. Also their sons Francis O'Neill who died 22nd July 1881, John O'Neill who died 26th Aug. 1905. O'Neill.   H

150. IHS. This stone was erected by Michael Bradley to the memory of Bridget O'Neill his wife who dep. this life 4th of Febry. in the 50th year of her age A.D. 1834. Requiescant in pace.   H

151. IHS. Here lieth the body of Shusana mcNeale who depd. this life Dec^{m}my^{e} 28th 1811 agd. 84 yrs. Also her son Brian mcNeal who depd. this life June the 21 1813 aged 57 yrs.   H

FLOWER VASE – Anne Toner Straw died 1st Dec 1954.

152. Erected in memory of John Hagen and Mary Hagen by their family. Also their aunt Bridget Hagen died 18th April 1920. H

153. Erected by Henry Toner in memory of his father John Toner who departed this life 14th April 1874 aged 64 years. Also his mother Ellen Toner who departed this life 9th April 1880 aged 66 years. Also his sister Ellen Toner who departed this life 26th Dec. 1884 aged 22 years. "Requiescant in Pace". H

154. STONE SURROUND – O'Connor Gortnaskea

155. IHS. Erected in memory of Laughlin Kelly who departed this life the 5th May 1855 aged 78 years. H

156. IHS. Erected in memory of Francis Groogan, who died 15th April 1835 aged 42 years. S

157. IHS. Erected by Arthur Devlin in memory of his daughter Mary who depd. this life on the 30th Dec. 1842 aged 28 years. S

158. Erected in memory of Peter Kelly who died 6th May 1840 aged 46 years, his wife Shibbie Kelly who died 4th Dec. 1862 aged 71 years. Also Rev. Patrick Kelly C.C. who died 5th Feb. 1860 aged 60 years. RIP. H

159. Our Lady of Lourdes pray for them. Erected in loving memory of James McBride who died 28th Jany. 1911 and his wife Jane McBride who died 17th Feby. 1920. Also their children. RIP. On whose souls sweet Jesus have mercy.   McBride.   H

160. IHS. Here lieth the body of patrick mcWilliams who dep. this life March the 1th 1818 agd. 58 yrs.   H

161. IHS. Here lieth the body of Ayls O hara otherways Flanagan who dpd. this life April the 7th 1821 aged 49 yrs.   H

ROW 15

162. IHS. Re-erected this centenary year 1953 to the memory of The Very Rev. Dr. O'Loughlin P.P., V.C. who was Parish Priest 1834-1860 and built Straw Church 1852-53. RIP.   H

163. In memory of Matthew McGlade of Cahore who departed this life the 29th October 1869 aged 40 years. John J. Rogers died 12th October 1904 aged 25 years. Susanna McGlade died 16th March 1861, John McGlade died 9th March 1880, Mary McGlade died 11th December 1883, Bernard Rogers died 9th October 1910 and his wife Rose died 12th March 1928.   Requiescant in Pace.   H

164. IHS. Erected by Charles O'Hagan, Drumderg in memory of his mother Ann O'Hagan who died 31st January 1871 aged 80 years.   H

165. IHS. Erected in memory of Patrick Kennedy who departed
      this life 4th August 1857 aged 76 yrs. Also his wife Bridget
      Kennedy who died 8th July 1863 aged 67 yrs. Also their
      daughter Teresa.   H

166. IHS. Charles Henery his wife Cathrine Henery who dpd.
      this life Decm. the 26th 1816 aged 48 yrs. Also his son
      Charles who dep. this life Augs. 17th 1812 aged 3 yrs.   H

167. IHS. Erected by Daniel Henry in memory of his wife
      Matilda who died 16th April 1837 aged 48 years. Also his
      son Pat who died 9th Janry. 1844 aged 27 years. The above
      Daniel Henry died 17th February 1864 aged 72 years.   H

168. IHS. Here lieth the body of Sarah Hart who depd. this life
      Septr. 30th 1816 agd. 40 yrs. Also her daughter Bridget
      McKenna who died April 15th 1825 agd. 22 yrs.   H

169. Erected by Mary O'Hagan in memory of her father Francis
      O'Hagan who died 26th Decr. 1862 aged 73 years. Also his
      son Francis who died 10th April 1849 aged 5 years.   H

170. IHS. Erected in memory of Peter Crilly who departed this
      life September 28th 1830 aged 56 years. Also his wife Ails
      Bradley died Aprail 29th 1840 aged 49 years.   H

171. Death the gate of eternal life.
Of your charity pray for James Kearney, Gortnaskea who died 28th October 1890 aged 80 years. Also his wife Mary who died 11th November 1889 aged 76 years. Their son James who died 26th April 1878 aged 36 years. Their son John who died 10th May 1888 aged 42 years. Their daughter Mary Ann O'Hagan who died 29th November 1893 aged 45 years. Their son Thomas who died 9th April 1915 aged 67 years. Their daughter Jane who died 21st August 1923 aged 65 years. Kearney.
Their grandsons Edward James O'Hagan who died 8th April 1895 aged 18 years. Laurence O'Hagan who died 18th Feb. 1912 aged 20 years. Thomas O'Hagan who died 11th Feb. 1917 aged 32 years.   H

172. IHS. Here lieth the body of John (Heggin) who departed this life . . . . . aged (15) yrs. Also his son Mick who dep. this life April 19th 1817 aged (19) yrs.   H

173. IHS. Erected by Francis Higerty in memory of his wife Bridget Higerty or otherwise Toner who dept. this life July the 17th 1833 aged 76 yrs.   H

174. Thy will be done.
Erected in memory of Mary Bradley died 18th January 1888 aged 65 years and her husband Charles Bradley died 13th June 1900 aged 87 years and their grand-daughter Kate Bradley died 13th August 1907 aged 23 years. Also their daughter Kate Bradley died 20th November 1939 and their son Patrick Bradley died 3rd August 1940. Bradley.   H

175. IHS. Here lieth the body of Michael O'Hagan who depd. this life 1st Febry. 1844 aged 60 yrs. Also his wife Bridget O'Hagan who died on the 1st August 1864 aged 74 years. H

ROW 16

176. IHS. In memory of Patrick Donnelly of Draperstown who died 12th March 1883 aged 50 years. Also his daughter Mary who died 7th March 1880 aged 4 years. "Requiescant in Pace". H

177. .... RIP. S

178. Memento Mori. IHS. Rev. Dean Murphy, Parish Priest of Ballinascreen for 30 years, died Feby. 24th 1834 aged 70 yrs. Requiescat in pace. S

179. Here lieth the body of the Revd. Patrick Morgan late pastor of the parish of Arsta and native of Ballinascreen who dep. this life June the 24th 1813 aged 53 years. S

180. IHS. Erected to the memory of Michl. Hagan who depd. this life the 17th of April 1827 aged 66 yrs. Also his wife Jane Hagan who depd. this life the 13th of Jany. 1813 aged 77 yrs. Also his daughter Jane O'Kane who depd. this life the 31st of Janry. 1839 aged 36 yrs. H

181. IHS. Patrick Mullan [   ] Also his daughter Sarah who depd. this life June 10 1814 aged 24 yrs. H

182. Thy will be done.
"Have pity on me. Have pity on me
At least you my friends"
Of your charity pray for the souls of Michael McKenna
who died 17th March 1877. His wife Mary McKenna who
died 4th June 1903. Their son Patrick McKenna who died
15th April 1884. Their son Peter McKenna who died 16th
February 1920 and is interred in Coleraine cemetery. Also
their daughter Rose A. McEldowney who died 4th Jan.
1921 and is interred in Drumagarner, Kilrea. On their
souls sweet Jesus have mercy. Also Annie McKenna died
21st Sep. 1922.   H

183. IHS. Erected by Daniel Mossey in memory of his wife
Ann Mossey who departed this life 14th Febry. 1839 aged
56 years.   S

184. In loving memory of Mary Mullan who died 14th June
1976.   Stone surround

185. IHS. Here lieth the body of Eles. Mellen otherwase
mcGugin who deped. this life Decr. 8th 1811 agd. 75 yrs. H

186. IHS. Here lieth the body of Henry Mallen who departed
this life 2nd August .... aged 35 years.   S

187. Erected in memory of Francis and Matilda McGlade, Moykeeran by their surviving sons.

A. Sarah Lynch wife of Francis McGlade junior died 13th September 1854 aged 32 years. Also Jane the daughter of Francis died 28th April 1894 aged 24.

B. Matthew McGlade son of Francis McGlade senior died 19th February 1851 aged 38 years. Also Matthew only son of the above Matthew McGlade died 17th March 1867 aged 16 years. Also his sister Margaret who died 21st Sept. 1880 aged 69 years and also her husband John Bradley who died 30th April 1889 aged 83 years and their son James who died 15th August 1876 aged 24 years.

C. Francis McGlade died 18th January 1872 aged 88 years. Also his wife Matilda McKenna died 17th January 1867 aged 80 years and their daughter Rose died 9th May 1850 aged 18 years. H

188. IHS. In memory of John McGlade of Tonaght who departed this life 19th August 1866 aged 80 years. Also of his wife Rose who died 23rd January 1883 aged 94 years. RIP. H

189. IHS. Here lieth the body of Matthew McGlade who departed this life Sept. the 16th 1811 aged 64 yrs. Also his son James McGlade who departed this life 6th Sept. 1840 aged 60.
Here lieth the body of the Rev. Patrick McGlade deceased 16th July 1843 aged 61 years. S

190. IHS. In memory of Charles McGlade, Cahore who died May 24th 1812 aged 73. Also his wife Mary McGlade who died Janyr. 19th 1844 aged 67. S

191. IHS. Erected in memory of John McGlade, Cahore who depd. this life Feby. 15th 1844 aged 47 yrs. Also his wife Betty McGlade who depd. this life Decr. 15th 1840 aged 39 yrs. H

192. IHS. Patrick McGlade of Tonagh died 22nd of March 1821 aged 62 years. Also his wife Martha McGlade alias Kelly died 8th of January 1853 aged 88 years. H

193. IHS. Here lieth the body of Laurence McGlade who departed this life June 30th 1817 aged 66 years. H

194. IHS. Erected to the memory of William Doogan who depd. this life 3rd Janry. 1810 aged 73 yrs. Also his wife Catherine Doogan who depd. this life 13th Dec. 1838 aged 72 yrs. Also his daughter Ann Connelly who depd. this life 4th Octr. 1836 aged 44 yrs. Also their daughter-in-law Nancy Doogan died 26th April 1884 aged 69 years. Also their son William Doogan died 18th Feby. 1896 aged 84 yrs. S

195. IHS. Erected by Owen McGlade in memory of his affectionate parents Phelimy McGlade who depd. this life March 24th 1835 aged 76 yrs. Also Jean McGlade (alias) Morran who depd. this life Novr. 26th 1833 aged 68 yrs. And Peter McGlade who depd. this life April 30th 1833 aged 38 yrs. H

196. IHS. Erected by James Morgan in memory of his wife Mary McCullough who died 11th April 1896.   H

197. Gloria in Excelsus Deo. Here lieth the body of John Rodgers who dep. this life March the 8th 1827 aged 61 years.   H

ROW 17

198.

A. In memory of James Henry who died 22nd October 1880 aged 67 years and his son James who died 18th October 1896 aged 50 years. Ellen Henry died 3rd October 1908 aged 80 years. Mary C. Henry born 28th February 1850 died 14th August 1918. Patrick Joseph Henry born 3rd January 1866 died 9th April 1919.   H

B. Michael Henry died 22nd April 1855 aged 75. Rose his wife 8 Feby. 1837 aged 50 years. Mary their daughter in law 12th June 1850 aged 29 years. Edward Henry died 21st Jany. 1879 aged 37 years.   H

199. Denis O'Hagan died 6th April 1841 aged 80. His wife Peggy Hasson 23rd May 1826 aged 52 years. Their son Hugh 5th Feby. 1865 aged 64 and his wife Catherine Murpmy [sic] 14th Feby. 1882 aged 87 years. Also their son John O'Hagan who died 6th January 1904 aged 73 years. John O'Hagan died 6th Jan. 1904. Patrick O'Hagan died 29th April 1915. The last of their race.   H

200. IHS. Erected by the Revd. James Murphy in memory of his father Patrick who lived regarded and died lamented July 19th A.D. 1827 aged 78 years. Also his brother Edward who died Feb. 12th 1834 aged 34 years. Here lie the remains of Margt. Murphy alias Henry who departed this life Nov. 15th 1821 aged 64 years. Requiescant in Pace. Amen   S

201. Erected in memory of Francis O'Neill who died 22nd May 1865 aged 10 years. Also his brother John O'Neill who died 12th April 1869 aged 5 years. His mother Elizabeth O'Neill who died 3rd December 1893 aged 59 years and his father Bernard O'Neill who died 28th October 1900 aged 71 years. Also Bernard O'Neill Jnr. who died 5th February 1926 aged 67 years.
O'Neill & Co. Sculptors, Belfast   H

202. Mary . . . .
Sarah . . . .   H(half broken)

203. Erected in memory of Patrick Thompson who departed this life 26th January 1838 aged 47 years.   S(half broken)

204. IHS. Erected by Jane Ryan (alias Crilly) in memory of her father John Crilly who departed this life 16th Mar. 1823 aged 47 years. Also her mother Catherine Crilly who departed this life 12th August 1831 aged 59 years. "Requiescant in Pace".   H

205. IHS. Erected in memory of Patrick Henry who departed this life 10th Augt. 1869 aged 80 years. Also his beloved wife Mary who departed this life 22nd Nov. 1858 aged 70 years. Also their son Patrick who departed this life 3rd July 1876 aged 40 years.   H

206. IHS. The burying place of John McNamee. Also the remains of Ann McNamee who depd. this life April 22nd 1831 in the 18th year of her age.   S

207. IHS. Sacred to the memory of Patrick Regan who departed this life May the 28th 1817 aged 86 years.   H

208. Erected by John Russell of New Zealand in loving memory of his father Robert Russell who died 23rd June 1872 aged 72 years. Also his mother Mary Russell who died 5th June 1878 aged 75 years. Also their children Hugh who died 10th Dec. 1882 aged 40 years, Jane who died 31st March 1890 aged 61 years. Here also lies the body of Michael Russell who died 12th Nov. 1818 aged 17 years. Requiescant in Pace. Russell.   H

209. IHS. Erected in memory of Dominick Groogan who departed this life 21st February 1859 aged 62 years. Also his daughter Sarah Groogan who departed this life 24th March 1874 aged 27 years. Also his wife Catherin Groogan who departed this life 17th January 1997 [Sculptor's mistake for 1897?] aged 86 years. May they rest in peace.
O'Neill, Divis St., Belfast   H

210. No inscription   Iron rails

211. No inscription   S

212. IHS. Here lieth the body of Barned McHugh aged 16
     years.   H

213. IHS. The burying place of Edward Ferris. Also William
     Friels died 22nd Dec. 1967.   H

213A. (Directly behind 213, along wall)
     IHS. Here lieth the body of Michael McNamee who
     departed this life January the 17th 1840 aged 72 years.   H

ROW 18
214. Headstone base

215. IHS. Erected by William Looney in memory of his wife
     Mary Anne Looney who died Novr. 18th 1881 aged 41
     years. RIP. Also his daughter Theresa Looney who died
     May 13th 1884 aged 20 years. RIP.   H

216. Bradley.   Stone surround

217. IHS. Isabella Quigley(alias) Conway died 27th February
     1869 aged 61 years. Also Patrick Quigley died 31st March
     1883 aged 88 years.   H

218. IHS. Here lieth the body of Teague McKenna who depd.
     this life Jan. the 9 1819 aged 63 years.   H

219. IHS. Erected by Daniel McKenna in memory of his wife Eleanor McKenna who died 3rd Octr. 18(30) aged 39 years. Also of their four children who died previous. Daniel McKenna died May . . . 18 . . . aged 40 years. RIP. Remodeld[sic] by H. McKenna, Kentucky, USA 1881.   S

220. IHS. Clerkin. In loving memory of our dear parents Joseph and Mary Clerkin, our grandparents Andrew and Catherine Clerkin and our niece and nephew. RIP. Erected by Paddy Clerkin and his sister Catherine.   H

Index to Names

Leyden – 92
Looney – 215
Loughran – 72, 73
Lynch – 39, 187
Magee – 16
Mallaghan(Stone mason) – 32
Mallen – 186
Mallon – 45
Mellen – 185
Moore – 126
Moran – 32, 106
Morgan – 179, 196
Morran – 195
Morren – 55
Mossey – 183
Mullan – 181, 184
Murphy – 178, 200
Murpmy – 199
Murray – 65, 66
Murry – 18, 94
Mury – 93
mcEldowney – 99
mcGugin – 185
mcNeal – 151
mcNeale – 151
mcWilliams – 160
McAllister – 28, 43
McAnally – 103
McBride – 39, 159
McCartney – 1
Mccloskey – 90

Index of Places

PREVIOUS BALLINASCREEN HISTORICAL SOCIETY PUBLICATIONS

1980   **'The Wee Black Tin'** (Poems by George Barnett and John 'Paul' Kelly   -out of print

1981   **'Ordnance Survey Memoir for Ballinascreen 1836-37'**
-out of print

1982   **'The Meetin House'** (Draperstown Presbyterian Church History)   -out of print

1983   **'Statistical Reports of Six Derry Parishes, 1821'**
(Ballinascreen, Kilcronaghan, Desertmartin, Boveva, Banagher, Dungiven)   -out of print

1984   **'Songs and Music of Ballinascreen'** (L.P, record & cassette)   -sold out

1985   **'Notes on the Placenames of Parishes and Townlands of the county of Londonderry'** by A. M. Munn, 1925 (Limited edition reprint)   -out of print

1986   **'Ordnance Survey Memoirs for the Parishes of Desertmartin and Kilcronaghan, 1836-1837'**
-out of print

1986   **'Images of Ballinascreen'** – V.H.S. video cassette
- sold out

1987   **'Famous Maghera Men'** by Eoin Walsh
-out of print

1988	**'The Heart of Ballinascreen'** – Poems by Nora Ni Chathain	-out of print

1988   **'The Heart of Ballinascreen'** – Poems by
      Nora Ni Chathain   -out of print

1989   **'Looking Back on Ballinascreen'** – A miscellany
      of writings relating to the district
           -out of print

1990   **'The Autobiography of Thomas Witherow, 1824-**
       1890'   -£8.95 inc. p&p

1991   **'In Crockmore's Shade'** – A selection of poems by
      John 'Paul' Kelly (1884-1944) of Doon, Draperstown
           -£3.50 inc. p&p

1992   **'John O'Donovan's letters from County**
      Londonderry (1834)' – letters containing information
      collected during the progress of the Ordnance Survey
           -out of print

1993   **'The Life and Adventures of Hudy McGuigan'**
      by Hugh Harkin   -£5.50 inc. p&p

1994   **'Gleanings from Ulster History'** by Seamus
      O' Ceallaigh(1879-1954)   -out of print

1995   **'Griffith's Valuation (1859) – Magherafelt Union'**
           -out of print

1996   **'The Big House – Derrynoyd Lodge, Draperstown'**
      Notes on the Torrens/O'Neill family and their former
      home, now site of The Rural College
           -out of print

1996   **'The McHenry Letters (1834-46)'** – Correspondence from Rev. J. L. McHenry of Culdaff, Co Donegal to his mother at Owenreagh, Draperstown   **-£5 inc. p&p**

1997   **'A Hospital at Magherafelt'**
Part 1 – The Workhouse and Famine times in South Derry   **-out of print**

1998   **'A Hospital at Magherafelt'**
Part 2 – The Workhouse – the final fifty years (1891-1941)   **-out of print**

1998   **'A Hospital at Magherafelt'**
Part 3 – The Hospital years – from 1941   **-£7.75 inc. p&p**

1999   **'Lewis's Loughinsholin (1837)'** – South Derry extracts from Samuel Lewis's *Topographical Dictionary of Ireland*   **-£5.60 inc. p&p**

2000   **'A Century makes Changes'** – Selected extracts from the South Derry & District Almanac 1902/1909   **-£5.00 inc. p&p**

2001   **'Shaw Mason's Maghera (1814) and Killelagh(1819)'**   **-£3.50 inc. p&p**

2002   **'Change and Decay'** – Bygone Buildings of Ballinascreen   **-out of print**

2003   **'The Churches of Ballinascreen'** A set of nine postcards   **-£4.00 inc. p&p**

2003   **'Ballinascreen'** by Mgr. J A Coulter (1919-1983)

-**£7.50 inc. p&p**

2004   **'Memorial Inscriptions'** – St Columba's & St Anne's
Churches

-**out of print**

2005   **'Those were the days!'** by Owen Kelly

-**out of print**

2006   **'A Generation of Montgomerys'** by Rt. Rev. Bishop Henry
Montgomery (1847 – 1932)   -**£5.75 inc. p&p**

2007   **'The Schools of Ballinascreen (1823 - 1990)'** by Fr. Leo
Deery, PP (1922-2002)

-**£7.65 inc. p&p**